Steamers to Rothesay

and the Isle of Bute

Andrew Clark

Queen Mary II at the east berth of Rothesay Pier in 1970.

First published in the United Kingdom, 2015,
by Stenlake Publishing Ltd.
Telephone: 01290 551122
www.stenlake.co.uk

ISBN 9781840337273

Acknowledgements

Photographs were kindly provided by A.E. Bennett, Ian Duncan, Graham Lappin, Fraser MacHaffie, Eric Schofield, David Scott, the J.T.A. Brown Collection and the estate of Walter and Effie Kerr. Images from the Geoffrey Grimshaw Collection are reproduced by courtesy of the Watt Library, Inverclyde Council, and those from the Roy Hamilton and John Thomas Collections by courtesy of the Clyde River Steamer Club. The photograph on page 34 is reproduced by permission of Judge Sampson Ltd, Hastings, which owns the copyright www.judges.co.uk. Additional help came from Stuart Craig, Charles McCrossan, Iain MacLeod and John Newth.

Rothesay Pier *circa* 1888, with *Guy Mannering* (left) and the twin-funnelled *Victoria*.

Introduction

The island resort that we first glimpse from the decks of *Argyle*, *Bute* or *Waverley*, sailing past Bogany Buoy into Rothesay Bay, does not look substantially different from how it was 50 or 100 years ago. The principal landmarks – the villas overlooking the water, the Pavilion, the esplanade – are much the same. So is the natural beauty of the setting. Looking out from Chapel Hill or Skipper's Wood in fine weather, you sense the magnificence of Bute and the timeless charm of its surroundings, with lochs, Kyles, promontories and peaks contained in a single sweep of the eye.

Nevertheless, a glance through the illustrations in this book reveals a different Rothesay to the unhurried town we know today. In its heyday, a period running from the 1870s to the 1970s, Rothesay had something for everybody: it was a microcosm of west of Scotland society, a characteristic summarised by its two nicknames, 'the Madeira of Scotland' and 'Glasgow by the sea'. Each had a contrasting emphasis. 'The Madeira of Scotland' speaks less of luxury than of middle-class prosperity, typified by the villas of Craigmore and the architectural quality of Rothesay's many churches. 'Glasgow by the sea' evokes memories not just of 'Paw, Maw and the weans', trailing prams and hampers as they descended on Rothesay for the Fair Fortnight, but of day-trippers who, for a few precious hours, exchanged the smoke and squalor of the city for the decks of a steamer and the delights of a Rothesay pub.

Was the Rothesay of yesteryear a richer place than it is today? In many respects, yes. The Winter Garden hosted the best Scottish entertainers. There were countless opportunities to take a trip round the bay or up the Kyles of Bute. As well as being a starting-point for ferries, carrying commuters to the mainland, the town was a picking-up point for sleek, speedy steamers. Holidaymakers had a fabulous choice of excursions, offering the chance to visit Arrochar, Ayr, Campbeltown or Inveraray and return in time for tea. Today, it is almost impossible to reach the neighbouring islands of Arran or Cumbrae without doing part of the journey by road.

This aspect of going to Rothesay for a holiday and using it as a base for exploring the Firth of Clyde by steamer has vanished, but the tension that once reigned between rowdyism and respectability – between inebriated trippers and genteel patrons of the Glenburn Hotel and Port Bannatyne's Hydropathic – is also, more happily, a thing of the past. The unsavoury element of the day trip from Glasgow, requiring a beefed-up police presence on Rothesay Pier, is long gone, even if *Waverley*'s Saturday crowd does its best to tell us otherwise.

That may be a sign of higher living standards, but it also reflects changing habits. Rothesay is not the hive of activity it was in the 1960s, when package holidays began to eat into its traditional clientele, offering Glaswegians guaranteed sun and exotic food at prices comparable to a fortnight on the Clyde. So it is hardly surprising that Bute's resident population today should stand at virtually half of what it was just over a century ago, when the Royal Burgh was at its most vibrant.

And yet, notwithstanding economic stagnation in the late 20th century, Rothesay's charms remain. It has managed to escape the soullessness to which many of Britain's other resorts have succumbed. Despite what some Brandanes may think, Bute still has excellent sea links to the mainland, with ferries no less elaborately built and fitted out than the magnificent pleasure steamers pictured in these pages.

Andrew Clark
Glasgow, July 2015

The 1860s saw the beginnings of Clyde steamer photography on an appreciable scale: this view from Chapel Hill dates from 1867 and shows the 1852 steamer *Venus* in the foreground, berthed next to the shipyard to the west of the harbour – a landmark that was removed in 1872, the year before *Venus* was broken up. The Wemyss Bay steamer *Argyle* lies at the main quay, which is in the process of enlargement, with wooden piles being constructed at the west end (centre left). Nearly 60 years after the advent of steam navigation, there is ample evidence, from the masts in the inner harbour and sails in the foreground, that sailing ships were still trading to Bute. The foundations of Rothesay's harbour date from the mid-18th century, when the long-established Royal Burgh was a fishing centre. It was not until the 1840s that it eclipsed Largs and the Ayrshire coast as the most popular destination for Glaswegians during the Fair.

Skipper's Wood, overlooking Rothesay Bay from the east, has long been a favoured vantage point for photographing comings and goings at the pier, for which it offers a more close-up view than Chapel Hill. By the early 1880s, when this picture was taken, a spacious promenade had been built on the west side of the bay and plans were afoot to replace the wooden pier buildings with something more substantial. The extension at the far end of the pier is clearly visible: its concave face presented difficulties for steamers berthing from the west, but it was not until 1899 that a longer convex pier, with three berths along the face, was created. This is a mid-morning portrait, with the Wemyss Bay steamer *Lancelot* in the foreground and, ahead of her, MacBrayne's Ardrishaig mail steamer *Iona*.

Captain Alexander Campbell's Wemyss Bay fleet poses for the camera in Rothesay Bay: the photograph was taken sometime between 1886, when the twin-funnelled *Victoria* (second from left) was launched, and 1889, the last year in which all four steamers operated on the Clyde. Two decades earlier Captain Campbell and his father-in-law, Captain James Gillies, had taken over the interests of the Wemyss Bay Steamboat Company, which in 1865 made an ill-fated attempt to operate steamers in connection with the new railway line to Wemyss Bay. *Argyle* (left) was one of the steamers taken over by the two captains, who added *Lancelot* (second from right) in 1875 and *Adela* (right) in 1877. By 1890 the Caledonian Railway's steamer-owning subsidiary had muscled in on the Wemyss Bay route, and all four steamers were sold off the Clyde.

Victorian elegance is the theme of this late afternoon portrait of Rothesay, captured at the height of summer in the early 1880s. While smartly dressed holidaymakers wander along the Esplanade, David MacBrayne's majestic *Columba* occupies the west berth of the pier. At 301 feet, *Columba* was the Clyde's longest steamer – a record she held for more than a century. From her debut in 1878 until her withdrawal in 1935 she called at Rothesay twice a day, six days a week in summer, on a journey that began at the heart of Glasgow shortly after 7am and took her to Ardrishaig and back – the first leg of the prestigious 'Royal Route', so named because of a visit to the West Highlands in 1847 by Queen Victoria and Prince Albert.

Most Clyde piers were built to serve coastal communities in an age when it was quicker and more convenient to travel by steamer than by horse and cart. Port Bannatyne, a village overlooked by Kames Castle, ancient home of the Bannatynes, was a case in point. The journey round the corner to bustling Rothesay may be a short one, but for the early Victorians those three miles represented a barrier. Until 1857, when its pier was opened by the Glasgow-Rothesay steamer *Mail*, Port Bannatyne made do with a stone quay, a tidal structure that could not attract the large and fast steamers on which the reputation of coastal villages increasingly depended. By the early 1900s, despite the inauguration in 1885 of a horse-drawn tramway to Rothesay (electrified in 1902), Port Bannatyne was attracting 20 calls a day and more at weekends, mostly from steamers en route to and from the Kyles of Bute. Regular visitors included the Glasgow and South Western Railway's *Mars* (above left) and *Minerva* (opposite page).

Opposite: *Marchioness of Bute* was a regular visitor to Kilchattan Bay throughout the 1890s, though she rarely deposited more than the coach load of passengers seen here preparing to set off along the shore road. Such scenes were common around the Clyde in the quarter-century before the First World War, when most communities had daily steamer links with a railhead. Given its modest size, Kilchattan Bay was particularly well served, with the Caledonian Steam Packet Company (CSP) providing a connection from Wemyss Bay and the Glasgow and South Western Railway from Fairlie, in both cases via Millport. *Marchioness of Bute* was a CSP boat, built in 1890 during the initial flurry of railway-financed steamer services on the Clyde. In 1908 she became surplus to requirements and was sold to owners on the Tay. She was broken up in 1923, but her sister, *Marchioness of Breadalbane,* continued on the Clyde until 1935.

Regatta day at Rothesay in the mid 1890s: stealing the limelight from the yachts are two paddlers bearing the yellow funnels of the Caledonian Steam Packet Company – *Galatea* (left) heading out of the bay with a good complement of passengers and *Marchioness of Breadalbane* (right) arriving with only a handful on deck. Both have an auxiliary foresail – a common feature on Clyde steamers until the early 1900s, though it was rare to see it opened out. *Galatea* was the first new vessel to join the CSP fleet when the Caledonian Railway's steamer-owning subsidiary burst upon the scene in 1889. Distinctive for her two widely spaced funnels, with her whistle unusually in front of the after one, she was placed on a daily cruise round Bute, supplemented in the mornings and evenings by commuter services to and from Gourock. Never quite the success her owners had hoped for, she was sold to Italian owners in 1906.

30421. ROTHESAY FROM WEST.

As a study of the Clyde in the palmy days of colour and competition, the scene on the opposite page could hardly be bettered: it shows Rothesay Pier in the summer of 1899, with finishing touches being put to an extension to the west end. It is 10.26am, but the crowds suggest it will be a while yet before the twin-funnelled *Columba* and *Lord of the Isles* can set off, a little late this morning, for another neck-and-neck race up the east Kyle en route to Loch Fyne. The North British excursion steamer *Redgauntlet* blows off steam in the foreground, while in the westernmost berth, wreathed in steam, is a 'Caley' steamer on ferry duty. The impression of a pier bustling with activity is equally well conveyed by the scene above, showing *Kylemore*, *Lord of the Isles* and *King Edward* in 1910.

J. Adamson and Son, the Rothesay photographers, occupy a special place in the annals of Clyde steamer history. From the 1880s to the 1930s Adamson created an outstanding library of ship photographs, captured on glass negatives and sold in beautifully textured prints. Adamson's images accentuated the beauty and line of the steamers – often against a backdrop of the hills above Loch Striven, as in this early 1890s portrait of the Glasgow and South Western Railway's *Glen Sannox*. Born in Lanarkshire, the original John Adamson (1820-1912) established himself at Rothesay in the early years of photography, initially with a studio in Victoria Street and later at 126 Sauchiehall Street, Glasgow, where he styled himself a 'photographic artist'. From 1873 he and his son, also John, worked predominantly in Rothesay, using their small steam yacht *Melita* as a platform for close-ups of the steamers and yachts in the bay. John junior later became sole owner of the business, but died of a 'malignant disease' in 1896 aged 44, leaving a widow and two infants. The business was sold, but its name continued even without the Adamson family's involvement. The new owners prolonged the 'house style' and made it more commercial, with a 1930s postcard series that still commands a second-hand market. The firm did not survive the Second World War, and the Adamson glass negative collection – paired with that of William Robertson, the Gourock photographer – is preserved in the Glasgow University archives.

Since 1865, when a railway connection with Glasgow was established, Wemyss Bay Pier has offered the shortest crossing for travel by train and boat to Rothesay. Its elegant structure, still largely intact today, dates from an enlargement carried out by the Caledonian Railway in 1903. Overlooked by a 60-foot clock tower, the station buildings were designed in Queen Anne style, with a magnificent covered walkway curving down to the centre-point of the pier, which had five steamer berths. In this picture the 1891 *Marchioness of Lorne* occupies what became known as the Rothesay berth.

'Heather Jock', standing in the foreground with peaked cap, was an itinerant, well known in the late 1890s in the resorts around the Firth, and particularly at Rothesay where he would sell purple heather with the cry "Heather, heather, fresh frae the hills to-day". His day began early with a trip to the hills to pick his supply for tourist steamers. A single bunch went for one penny, but a prized tuft of "lucky white heather" would fetch a premium – sixpence at least, or even a shilling if the purchaser happened to be an English or American tourist. All through the summer Jock pursued his trade and did good business with the crowds of eager excursionists, who tossed him coppers and received in exchange a bunch of fragrant purple heather.

The 1899 extension to the west end of Rothesay Pier made it possible for three large steamers to berth along the face of the pier, while also creating an inside berth, occupied here by the cargo steamer *Bute 4*. The paddler on the outside berth is the Caledonian Steam Packet Company's *Duchess of Rothesay*, one of the most beautifully proportioned of all Clyde steamers. With smoke drifting lazily from *Bute 4*'s funnel and little activity on the pier, Rothesay seems at peace with itself. You would never guess that this photograph was taken a fortnight before the world went to war in July 1914.

The Glasgow and South Western Railway's Ayr excursion steamer *Juno* makes a handsome sight at Port Bannatyne Pier. Built at Clydebank in 1898, she achieved 19.26 knots on trial and was more heavily built than most Clyde paddlers of her day, making her well suited to the open sea. Her summer timetable took her as far afield as Stranraer to the south and Arrochar to the north, but she also visited many of the Firth's smaller piers. On 18th August 1922, for example, she left Ayr at 10am and reached Port Bannatyne at 2.20pm, having sailed via Troon, Ardrossan, Keppel, Largs, Garroch Head and the Kyles of Bute. The return journey began at 4pm and she was back in Ayr shortly before 7pm.

For the best part of 30 years – six days a week, winter and summer – *Kylemore* would leave Rothesay in the morning for Glasgow and return down-river in the afternoon, carrying a mixed load of passengers and cargo. It was a plodding sort of role for a Clyde steamer, and her crew were not as immaculately turned-out as their counterparts on the glamorous excursion steamers. Nevertheless, *Kylemore* 'belonged' to Rothesay in a way no other steamer did, berthing overnight on the inside of the west end of the pier – officially designated as Berth 1A, but known as 'the Kylemore berth' (see page 24). This photograph from the 1920s, when *Kylemore* was owned by Williamson-Buchanan Ltd, shows her lying across the end of the pier, with the North British Railway Company's *Waverley* on the left. When she joined the war effort in November 1939 *Kylemore* was already more than 40 years old. Nine months later she was sunk by a German plane off the south-east coast of England.

In the mid to late 19th century Craigmore established itself as the upmarket suburb of Rothesay, an impression underlined by the spacious layout of the sea-front in this photograph from 1922, showing the tennis club and a substantial pier building. The pier, dating from 1877, was an ornate iron structure with a conventional timber face. Its main purpose was to serve commuters, many of them businessmen who would leave their family in one of Craigmore's elegant villas in summer and travel up and down to Glasgow during the week. The steamer at the pier is the Caledonian Steam Packet Company's *Duchess of Rothesay*, bearing the distinctive 'Caley' livery of black hull and all-yellow funnel. She is probably on a run from Gourock or Wemyss Bay, while the Glasgow and South Western Railway's *Glen Rosa* (lavender hull, red-and-black-top funnel) is passing on her way from Millport or Largs. Both ships were built at Clydebank in the 1890s. *Duchess of Rothesay* survived the Second World War but was broken up immediately afterwards. *Glen Rosa* was broken up in 1939 just before war was declared.

Only six years separate this 1928 picture of Craigmore Pier from the view on the previous page, but a significant change had taken place, illustrated by the livery of *Mercury*. Like *Glen Rosa* she had worn the colours of the Glasgow and South Western Railway throughout her early career, but in 1923 the G&SW fleet was merged with the 'Caley' under the umbrella of the London Midland and Scottish Railway (LMS), a move dictated by post-war rationalisation. For that year alone, the combined fleet maintained their existing hull colours while funnels became a compromise of yellow with black top, separated by a red band. These 'tartan lums' were kept for 1924, when former G&SW steamers exchanged their lavender hulls for black, and from 1925 yellow-and-black became the standard funnel colouring for all LMS steamers. It was the first step in a process that saw less competition, and less colour, on the Clyde.

Rothesay Pier in summer has always been a barometer of fashion, and there is no mistaking the 1920s in this scene featuring *Queen Alexandra*, bound for Inveraray on 7th August 1926. Built by Denny of Dumbarton in 1912, the second Clyde turbine to bear the name, she was one of the longest and fastest steamers on the Firth. *Queen Alexandra* formed part of the white-funnelled fleet of Turbine Steamers Ltd, a privately owned business that dominated the Clyde's long-distance cruise market. When the company was dissolved in the mid 1930s, *Queen Alexandra* was bought by David MacBrayne Ltd as a replacement for the veteran paddler *Columba* on the summer mail run to Ardrishaig, for which she was renamed *Saint Columba*.

One of the earliest recorded instances of a car being offloaded from a Clyde steamer was at Dunoon in the late 1890s, from the paddle steamer *Benmore*. By the 1930s, when this photo was taken at Rothesay's Berth No. 3, the practice was, if not commonplace, then a regular occurrence – usually involving a turbine steamer with open deck space aft (here the 1925 *Glen Sannox*), or one of the paddlers that had been designed with a roomy area behind the funnel. Under the supervision of deck crew and pier staff, the owner drove the vehicle up two planks, with wooden wedges placed at the end to ease the path onto the deck. This is how it was done until the 1950s: it is only with hindsight, from the comfort of today's car ferries, that we look back aghast at the precariousness of it all. In the first half of the 20th century, vehicle traffic by steamer was limited not only by the inconvenience of the procedure but also by the fact that car ownership was beyond the means of most people.

The Winter Garden, a cast iron and glass structure pre-fabricated in Glasgow and erected in the centre of Rothesay's Esplanade Gardens in 1923-24, became a favourite entertainment venue for holidaymakers in the inter-war and post-war eras. But it's what lies beyond that catches the eye here. The photograph dates from the early 1930s, when the world was hit by an economic slump and Rothesay Bay became a dumping ground for out of work vessels. There was, however, no shortage of work for *Kylemore*, sitting at her inside berth at the west end of the pier, or for *Jeanie Deans*, the London and North Eastern Railway's long distance excursion steamer, whose forward funnel is obscured by the Winter Garden's turret. In its heyday the Winter Garden hosted variety performances by Harry Lauder, Jimmy Logan and Johnny Beattie. Closed in 1974 and threatened with demolition, the building was taken in hand by a trust and restored. Since 2001 it has been home to the Isle of Bute Discovery Centre, incorporating a 90-seat cinema theatre.

Queen Mary (centre) was the last steamer to be ordered for the 'doon the watter' trade. In the course of a Clyde career that ran from 1933 to 1977, she gave pleasure to generations of Glaswegians, the majority of whom disembarked at Rothesay and rejoined her later in the day for the return trip to the city. In the 1930s she left Glasgow at 10am and, after calls at Rothesay and other resorts, gave a non-landing cruise to the Arran coast. In the post-war era she was best known for her 11am sailing, seven days a week in summer, from Glasgow to Rothesay and Tighnabruaich. This picture dates from the late 1930s, after she had been renamed *Queen Mary II* (the suffix 'II' having been added in deference to the Cunard transatlantic liner, launched at Clydebank in 1934). One of the turbine 'Duchesses' sits on the left of the picture, and the pier's magnificent clock tower, flanked by baronial turrets, is on the right. Erected in 1885 the clock tower became one of the Clyde's best-loved landmarks, but was destroyed by fire in 1962.

Wartime grey imposed a dull monochrome on the Clyde fleet. Shallow-draught paddle steamers were converted into minesweepers and deployed hundreds of miles from home. Some never returned. Turbine steamers that had been built to take holidaymakers on summer cruises stayed on the Clyde, providing essential ferry services from the railheads. It was a humdrum existence, but it was relatively safe. Late in 1939 an anti-submarine boom was laid between the Cloch and Dunoon, dividing the Firth into two distinct areas: five years were to pass before Rothesay would be reconnected to Dunoon and the upper-firth railheads. *Duchess of Montrose* (left) and *Marchioness of Graham* (right) spent much of the war, summer and winter, running between Wemyss Bay and Rothesay.

The 1939-45 war took steamers to unlikely places. In peacetime *Marchioness of Graham* (left) was hardly a stranger to Rothesay, but she was more commonly found on the Ardrossan-Arran station. The real interloper here is *Loch Aline*, sitting in the Kylemore berth (right). Launched at Bowling in 1904 as *Plover*, she was an unexceptional passenger-and-cargo boat that had spent most of her life plying on David MacBrayne Ltd's Oban-Barra run. It was while on that service that, towards the end of the First World War, she had the distinction of fighting off a German submarine west of Tiree, using a single small gun at her stern. In 1934 she was substantially altered at Ardrossan for use as an excursion and tour boat in the West Highlands – complete with new name, extended promenade deck, hull painted half white and all yellow funnel. It is in this condition – in her wartime role as Rothesay-based examination vessel – that she is pictured in April 1940. The 'Graham' still has a yellow and black funnel, but later that year both ships were painted grey.

In the immediate post-war era *Caledonia* occasionally deputised as Millport steamer, a role that took her to Kilchattan Bay – viewed from the paddler's port sponson by Millport photographer Walter Kerr in the early 1950s. By this time the village on the south-eastern part of Bute was finding it hard to justify itself as a port of call. The canny company which ran the pier had never actually made a loss, probably because of the goods traffic that passed through its hands, but in 1949 cargo steamers stopped calling and the number of passengers using the connection to the mainland via Millport began to dwindle: it was now simpler to go by road to Rothesay and then by ferry to Wemyss Bay.

Marchioness of Lorne, pictured at Kilchattan Bay in 1953, served as Millport steamer for only one summer before being withdrawn: two years after this photograph was taken, she was broken up at Port Glasgow. Built at Fairfield's Govan yard in 1935 for the Holy Loch run out of Gourock, she was a remarkably neat little ship. The gold lines round her hull, the varnished wood of the bridge, the sense of proportion created by masts, windows and portholes – she almost looked like a paddle steamer in miniature. Her downfall was her speed – or rather, the lack of it. Cumbrae folk complained that they had been given a cast-off, and *Marchioness of Lorne* was duly taken off the run and laid up. *Talisman* became Millport steamer in 1954, maintaining the Kilchattan Bay connection until September 1955, when the pier closed due to falling traffic. Even so, in that year *Talisman* called 113 times, *Maid of Skelmorlie* 90 times, *Maid of Cumbrae* 11 times, *Caledonia* twice and *Jupiter*, *Waverley* and the car ferry *Arran* once each. In addition there were calls by 10 puffers.

In the late 1950s the British Prime Minister, Harold Macmillan, told voters they had "never had it so good". Before car ownership and package holidays became common, the crowds who swept through the station concourse and onto the pier at Wemyss Bay might well have agreed. Post-war living standards had risen steadily. The national railway system took holidaymakers to the far corners of the country, and the Clyde coast was enjoying a resurgence. Almost everyone in this picture will have arrived by train and be heading for Rothesay. It was a ritual followed by generations of Glaswegians, eager for the open waters of the Firth and the pleasurable diversions of their favourite resort. We can only imagine the sense of anticipation, bordering on excitement, felt by these people as they headed down the covered walkway, with the sound of waves beneath its timbers, and onto the open pier, where the steamer would be waiting, smoke curling from the funnel, to take them to Bute.

One of the steamers most commonly found at Wemyss Bay Pier in the post-war era was *Jupiter*, seen here in the Rothesay berth on 4th August 1951. Built in 1937, she was a workhorse, designed to ferry large numbers of passengers across the Firth rather than undertake excursions. On this occasion it looks as if even her generous capacity will not be enough to cope: the steamer from which the photograph was taken – berthed at the very end of the pier – is evidently acting as a back-up on one of the summer's peak Saturdays. *Jupiter* was withdrawn in 1957, just after she had been expensively converted from coal- to oil-burning. Wemyss Bay lost its five-berth pier in the late 1970s when tubular steel piles replaced the old timber structure, and a linkspan was fitted to what had previously been the Millport berth, just out of sight on the right of the picture.

Cross-channel turbine steamers made an impressive sight on their rare visits to Rothesay. They brought day-trippers from Belfast (usually on one of the Isle of Man Steam Packet Company's ships) or, as on this occasion on 24th June 1951, from Stranraer. The vessel towering over the west end berth is *Princess Margaret*, built at Dumbarton in 1931 for the Stranraer-Larne run, on which she served until 1961. *Jupiter* (left) is at the east end of the pier. The paddler preparing to take up the middle berth is *Caledonia* (right), whose skipper must have assumed she could berth before *Princess Margaret* left. Although the manner of her approach seems odd, it was a common manoeuvre for paddlers at Rothesay whenever space was tight: turning in towards the pier, they would 'slide' into a position roughly parallel to it, before paddling astern into the berth.

Seven new diesel ferries joined the Clyde fleet in 1953-54, as part of a modernisation plan designed to reduce costs and meet the changing needs of the travelling public. Three of these vessels were car ferries, and the camera has captured two at Rothesay on 28th August 1961 – *Arran* at the middle berth and *Bute* departing for Wemyss Bay. Dubbed the ABC ferries (the third was *Cowal*), they had garage space for 16 cars, later increased to 34, and a lift extending the full width of the hull just aft of midships, making the routine shipment of cars possible at existing piers. The lift was brought up or down to whatever level the tide required, a ramp was lowered and vehicles were driven on and off the side of the vessel. There was no need for pier modifications: car-carrying sailings could be fully integrated into the existing passenger timetable. The ABCs were fast and beamy, and traffic to Bute boomed.

The sun-blessed charm of a summer's morning at Rothesay is captured by this Judges' postcard from the late 1950s. *Duchess of Hamilton* (immediately behind the pier's clock tower) has just cast off from the west berth, bound for Campbeltown. An ABC ferry unloads at the middle berth and will shortly leave for Wemyss Bay. MacBrayne's *Lochfyne*, bound for Ardrishaig, is about to move astern into the east berth. *Gay Queen* sits on the other side of the bay at her jetty opposite the Pavilion. In some senses the scene is timeless. The comings and goings along the waterfront at Rothesay have always cast a spell. The ships and the people may have changed, but the spell continues to this day.

Toward Lighthouse (right), completed in 1812, the year of the Clyde's first steamship, has been a reassuring landmark for generations of travellers to Rothesay – especially in fine weather, when the white buildings on the foreshore gleam in the sun. In stormy conditions the waters off the lighthouse become a battle-ground between ship and wind. Everyone on board *Maid of Cumbrae* on 14th August 1959 will have been aware of that as she rounded Toward Point, shouldering the waves on her bow quarter. The 'Cumbrae' and the other three 'Maids', built in 1953 as part of the post-war fleet modernisation programme, were good sea boats, equally useful for basic services in winter and short cruises in summer. All four remained in service until the 1970s, with the 'Cumbrae' latterly being converted for use as a car ferry. Sold to Italy in 1978, she survived until 2006.

Manoeuvring astern into Berth 1A – Rothesay's 'Kylemore berth' – required skill, and Donald MacLeod, *Countess of Breadalbane*'s skipper, knew exactly how to do it. Built in 1936 to provide tourist trips on Loch Awe, the 'Breadalbane' was transferred in 1952 to the Clyde, where she undertook a variety of work. In the early 1960s this included the 4.50pm run from Craigendoran to Rothesay on summer Wednesdays, a service undertaken on other days of the week by a 'Maid' or a paddler. The 'Breadalbane', a smaller and slower vessel, usually managed to maintain their schedule, because MacLeod was so quick at piers. After arriving at Rothesay, she would proceed to the Kyles for what was advertised as an evening cruise, though its main purpose was to complete the circuit for passengers who had joined the Wednesday Arran via the Kyles steamer at Tighnabruaich in the morning. The 'Breadalbane' sported a white hull on the Clyde from 1961 to 1964.

Wemyss Bay Pier on 28th August 1965: *Maid of Argyll* lies at the Millport berth while *SRN6-010*, the Clyde's first hovercraft, boards passengers on the foreshore. Both were bound for Rothesay, with fares on the hovercraft being collected in a biscuit tin. That summer saw two hovercraft operating on the Clyde, each capable of carrying 38 passengers at speeds far greater than conventional ships. Registered in the name of Tarbert-based Clyde Hover Ferries, they were an interesting experiment which never really took off. They made a lot of noise, which provoked complaints from residents in the resorts they served, and they had problems with winter weather. Amid mounting losses they were withdrawn at the end of the year.

Halcyon days: *Caledonia, Queen Mary II* and *Marchioness of Graham* congregate in Rothesay Bay in 1949, with Toward Lighthouse across the water on the right, a pair of naval ships at anchor on the left and a church clock in the foreground indicating the time is 12.35pm. On the surface all is well with the world. After the years of wartime grey, colour had returned to the Clyde. Although wartime rationing was still in force, Rothesay and the other resorts were back in business. Behind the atmosphere of peace and wellbeing lay economic pressures that were to change the nature of the Clyde steamer trade, and the resorts they served, over the following 20 years. A year after railway nationalisation in 1948, the Clyde fleet was ill-equipped to deal with the demands of post-war Britain. It consisted mainly of passenger steamships, with large crews and even larger fuel bills – too large for the year-round trade they catered for. In 1949 the Caledonian Steam Packet Company, the steamer-operating subsidiary of British Railways, lost £95,000, an all-time record. By the end of the year passenger fares had been increased by 10 per cent and plans laid for a new generation of diesel ships that would reduce costs and provide greater flexibility.

As Millport steamer from 1954 until her withdrawal in 1967, *Talisman* made a daily visit to Rothesay on her summer afternoon 'Cumbrae Circle' cruise, which involved a call at Largs on her outward journey and a return to Millport 'via Kilchattan Bay' – part of the cruise that continued to be advertised long after the pier there closed in 1955. Technically speaking *Talisman* was not a steamer: she was built in 1935 with diesel-electric machinery, the only Clyde paddler to be powered in this way. Pictured shortly after radar was fitted in 1960, she looks in peak condition.

In 1963 and 1964 *Duchess of Montrose* and *Duchess of Hamilton*, the Clyde's two fastest steamers, engaged in a series of legendary races across the Firth of Clyde on Friday mornings. Both were due to leave Rothesay at 10.15am for Largs, with the 'Montrose' then heading for Campbeltown and the 'Hamilton' for Ayr. The races were unofficial, and the 'Montrose' never actually overtook her younger sister, but there were some close calls for the 'Hamilton', with clouds of smoke emanating from both steamers on the way across. This 'clash of the Clyde's best' came about because, after an unimpressive period in the 1940s and 1950s under a succession of masters, the 'Montrose' was commanded in 1963-64 by Captain John MacLeod, who shook things up. The older boat reacted positively to his attention, so that Captain Fergus Murdoch, skipper of the 'Hamilton' since 1946, had to start looking over his shoulder. These were handsome steamers, capable of more than 20 knots when new in the early 1930s, and the excitement on board as the two headed out of Rothesay Bay was palpable. The 'Montrose' was withdrawn at the end of the 1964 season, the 'Hamilton' (opposite page) in 1970.

DUCHESS OF HAMILTON
3

By the 1960s *Queen Mary II* was the sole surviving 'doon the watter' steamer. Every day in summer at 2.05pm she would disgorge hundreds of Glaswegians onto the pier at Rothesay, sometimes requiring extra gangways – as on this occasion, when the foredeck was opened up. *Queen Mary II* had a particular air of spaciousness, with an expanse of upper deck running from forward of the bridge to within a few feet of the stern. Her name reverted to *Queen Mary* in her last two seasons (1976-77), following the retirement of the Cunard liner of the same name. Between 1981 and 2008 she was used as a static restaurant on the Thames. In recent years a not-for-profit organisation, Friends of TS Queen Mary, has campaigned for her return to the Clyde.

Maid of Bute was one of two wooden pleasure boats giving cruises out of Rothesay in the post-war era, independent of the Clyde steamer fleet. Built at Fraserburgh in 1938 and owned by John Knox, she was a jolly little craft with a toy funnel and a decent turn of speed, which she put to good use on summer trips from the Inner Harbour to the Kyles of Bute. She was sold to Fort William in 1973 and later the Firth of Forth and the Thames, before moving in 1998 to Falmouth in Devon and St Mawes in Cornwall.

MacBrayne's Royal Mail steamer *Saint Columba* called at Rothesay twice a day in summer en route to and from Ardrishaig, usually berthing at the east end of the pier in the morning and the west end in the afternoon. Built as the twin-funnelled *Queen Alexandra* in 1912, she was bought by MacBraynes late in 1935 and transformed into the Clyde's only three-funneller. This photograph, showing *Arran* and a 'Maid' further along the pier, dates from 1957, the year before *Saint Columba* was broken up.

Gay Queen, pictured in the Narrows at the Kyles of Bute in 1966, became an unmistakable feature of Rothesay's holiday scene in the 1950s and 1960s, thanks to her singing skipper, Herbert McIver, and a distinctive red colour scheme. Of similar size to *Maid of Bute* but without a funnel, she offered a variety of cruises from a jetty opposite the Pavilion. By the 1980s, thanks to the proliferation of the motor car and package holidays, the market for short sea trips out of Rothesay had all but disappeared. Named in an era when 'gay' meant happy, *Gay Queen* was sold to the south of England in 1988. Renamed *Alice Marie* and later *Queen of the Fal*, she was reunited with her former rival *Maid of Bute* at Falmouth.

The Albert Pier lay at the extreme east end of Rothesay Harbour, disconnected from the main structure. Built in the early 1860s and extended in 1908-09, it was used by Clyde steamers only as a lay-by berth – as in this picture from 29th March 1970, showing *Keppel* (foreground) next to the coaster *Dawnlight 1*. *Keppel* was an occasional visitor to Rothesay from the time she joined the Clyde fleet in 1967 until her departure in 1995 for a new career in Malta. She was used mainly on the Millport-Largs passenger service, but her first Clyde skipper, Donald MacLeod, lived in Rothesay and missed no opportunity to spend the night there – especially on winter Sundays such as this, when she had the day off. Built in 1961 as a Thames ferry, *Keppel* boasted several unusual design features: her mast doubled as the exhaust for her diesel engine, and she was the first vessel on the Clyde to operate with Voith-Schneider propulsion, making her exceptionally manoeuvrable. For her last few years on the Firth she found employment as a cruise boat, for which her roominess proved useful – offsetting the fact that she was rather slow.

King George V sweeps gracefully past the Colintraive-Rhubodach ferry on her way down the East Kyle in 1971. Built in 1926 for Turbine Steamers Ltd's long-distance cruises from the upper Firth to Campbeltown and Inveraray, she was a familiar sight at Rothesay in her first 10 years of service: at that time her funnels were painted white with black top. In 1936 she joined the fleet of David MacBrayne Ltd and, with the lower part of her funnels painted red, began an illustrious career as Iona cruise steamer, operating out of Oban. Between 1970 and her withdrawal at the end of the 1974 summer, she gave a series of early season cruises on the Clyde, and it is in this guise that she is pictured. *King George V* had a distinguished war record, helping to evacuate British servicemen from Dunkirk in 1940, and became one of the most popular pleasure steamers of the post-war era.

When the car ferry service between Colintraive and Rhubodach was inaugurated in 1950, it was a primitive affair, comprising a former landing craft and a 'slipway' consisting only of wire matting on the beach. In 1969 the Caledonian Steam Packet Company took over the service from the Bute Ferry Company, and converted one of its Skye ferries, *Portree*, for the route: she is seen here in the mid 1970s with Colintraive in the background. Despite *Portree*'s increased capacity, the crossing remained cumbersome because, as a bow-loader, she had to reverse and swivel round every time she made the five-minute journey. The service did not become drive-through until 1986, when Caledonian MacBrayne introduced its new double-ended 'Loch' class ferries. Pictured on the left here is Leo Vogt, a founding member of the Clyde River Steamer Club in 1932 and later its honorary president.

On 9th August 1969 *Gourockian* visited Port Bannatyne on a steamer enthusiasts' charter. It was made possible by repairs in 1962 to a pier that, since the Second World War, had been bypassed by the Clyde steamer fleet. Port Bannatyne's heyday was before the First World War. The pier's last flourish of activity was in the mid 1930s, thanks to the initiative of a new pier master and the efforts of the local MP. The summer of 1936 saw 14 steamer calls on weekdays, plus visits by evening cruise steamers. When war was declared in 1939, Port Bannatyne became the first of Bute's satellite piers to go out of use: the 1937 *Jupiter* made the last scheduled call. *Gourockian*'s visit in 1969 was probably the only occasion she was seen there. Built in 1938 as *Ashton*, she and her sister, *Leven*, were among the first generation of diesel vessels on the Clyde, best remembered as the 'wee ferries' on the Millport-Largs service in the post-war era. Bought in 1965 by Roy Ritchie for ferry work from Gourock, she was renamed *Gourockian* three years later. Sold off the Clyde in 1971, she moved to Doncaster in 1978, where she still operates river cruises under the name *Wyre Lady*.

In the first half of the 20th century, the sight of three steamers berthed simultaneously at Rothesay was commonplace in summer, with the pier acting as a hub for cruise steamers and service boats heading in different directions. This photograph, taken on 4th September 1976, captures the end of an era. A year later the turbine steamer *Queen Mary* (left) was withdrawn from service. Although the car ferry *Glen Sannox* (centre) and the preserved paddle steamer *Waverley* (right) continued to call, Rothesay was never again to see three major units of the Clyde fleet congregating in this way.

In the mid 1970s *Glen Sannox* and *Queen of Scots* became a familiar sight at Rothesay Pier. Long a favourite on the Arran run, for which she had been built in 1957, the 'Sannox' proved less popular with the people of Bute: recurring mechanical problems led to poor time-keeping on the Wemyss Bay-Rothesay service. In June 1977, following her re-engining, she had the distinction of inaugurating the side-loading linkspan at Rothesay, and for the following four summers served as a CalMac cruise boat. *Queen of Scots*, built in 1935 as *Coronia* (later *Bournemouth Queen*), had a colourful Clyde career between 1974 and 1982 – initially ferrying workers to Sir Robert McAlpine's oil platform yard at Ardyne on the Cowal peninsula, and in 1977 deputising for *Waverley* after the paddler was stranded on the Gantocks off Dunoon. This picture was taken at the east end of Rothesay Pier in 1975.

Rothesay may be 'Scotland's Madeira', but the sun does not always shine, as this snow-strewn view from 6th January 1979 testifies. It shows *Arran*, the Clyde's first purpose-built car ferry, which became a familiar sight at Rothesay soon after her debut in 1953. Constructed as a side-loader, she was converted in 1973 to stern-loading, a move that radically altered her profile. The removal of her aft superstructure reduced the weight on her stern, affecting her stability: the crew quickly learned to position the biggest loads on the aft of the car deck, thereby helping to increase the grip of her propellers in the water. During reconstruction her funnel was given a cosmetic extension (known as a cowl), giving rising to the quip "the *Arran* has a beaut of a cowl" – a play on the names of her sister ships *Bute* and *Cowal*. *Arran* was the last of the three to be withdrawn, in 1979. Sold for use as a floating restaurant in Dublin, and later Manchester, she was broken up in 1993.

On 2nd September 1989 *The Second Snark* made a special visit to Kerrycroy on Bute's eastern shore. The village was never big or important enough to justify a steamer call, but in the 1880s and 1890s its stone pier played a role in the reconstruction of Mount Stuart, the Marquess of Bute's Gothic Revival mansion located a mile to the south. Stone and other materials for the new building were landed at Kerrycroy and taken by horse-drawn railway to Mount Stuart. *The Second Snark*'s call was organised by the Clyde River Steamer Club, which specialises in creating unusual opportunities for enthusiasts to sail together, and on the same day she visited disused piers at Kilchattan Bay, Portencross and Keppel. Built in 1938 by William Denny and Sons, the Dumbarton shipbuilder, as a tender for its new ships, the vessel has been owned since 1969 by Clyde Marine Motoring Ltd.

A jam-packed *Saturn* departs Rothesay on 31st May 1986. To the left is the airport-style pier building, opened in 1968 by Her Majesty the Queen Mother and replaced in 1992 by the more traditional structure in use today. To the right is the side-loading linkspan, inaugurated in 1977, which made possible a more fluent vehicle-loading and unloading operation than had previously been possible. Immediately behind *Saturn*'s stern ramp are the pier's world-renowned Victorian public conveniences, an ornately-tiled facility commissioned by Rothesay Harbour Trust in 1899 and beautifully restored in the 1990s.

Pioneer (left) leaves for Wemyss Bay with a supermarket lorry occupying the entire aft section of her car deck, while *Saturn* (right) prepares to berth. Built for the Islay run in 1974, *Pioneer* became a familiar sight at Rothesay between the mid 1990s and her departure from the fleet in 2004: she was one of CalMac's fastest and most versatile units, regularly serving on Clyde ferry runs and occasionally acting as cruise boat. It is the latter function that *Saturn* was fulfilling on 26th August 1997. She left Largs with a respectable number of passengers, pirouetted in Rothesay Bay while *Pioneer* finished loading and then, after a brief stop, proceeded up the Kyles of Bute. Built in 1978, originally with the words 'Rothesay Ferry' emblazoned across her hull, *Saturn* proved a useful member of CalMac's Clyde fleet until her withdrawal in 2011. In 2015 she was bought by the Orkney-based Pentland Ferries and renamed *Orcadia*.

The original *Vital Spark* was a puffer invented by Inveraray-born author Neil Munro (1863-1930). Captained by the redoubtable Para Handy, this fictional little steamboat came to symbolise the comedy of life aboard a type of vessel that proliferated in the west of Scotland in the late 19th and early 20th centuries, providing a vital supply link to isolated communities. The diesel-driven *Vital Spark* pictured here, at the east end of Rothesay Pier on Bute Games Day 2006, was built at Hull in 1944 for the Royal Navy as *VIC 72*. Rescued from an uncertain fate in the 1990s, she later became a museum exhibit at Inveraray. Behind her, *Waverley* is offloading a capacity crowd from Glasgow, while the car ferry *Bute* arrives from Wemyss Bay.